AMERICAN WOMEN SPIES OF WORLD WAR II

SIMONE PAYMENT

The Rosen Publishing Group, Inc., New York

Published in 2004 by The Rosen Publishing Group, Inc.
29 East 21st Street, New York, NY 10010

Library of Congress Cataloging-in-Publication Data

Payment, Simone.
American women spies of World War II/by Simone Payment.
   p. cm.—(American women at war)
Summary: Describes the lives and covert operations of six women who worked as American spies during World War II. Includes bibliographical references and index.
ISBN 0-8239-4449-2 (library binding)
1. World War, 1939–1945—Secret service—United States—Juvenile literature. 2. Women spies—United States—Biography—Juvenile literature. 3. Espionage, American—Europe—History—20th century—Juvenile literature. 4. Espionage, American—Philippines—History—20th century—Juvenile literature. [1. World War, 1939–1945—Secret service. 2. Spies. 3. Women—Biography. 4. Espionage.]
I. Title: American women spies of World War 2.
II. Title: American women spies of World War Two. III. Title.
D810.S7P395 2004
940.54'8673'0922—dc22

                                                          2003014696

Manufactured in the United States of America

On the front cover: Two female intelligence analysts work code machines during World War II.
On the back cover: An easy-to-conceal Liberator pistol

Contents

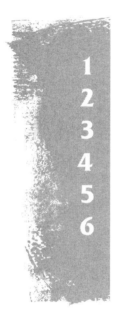

INTRODUCTION

Spies have been used in times of war and peace since the beginning of civilization, and women have long been involved in these espionage pursuits. In the United States, female spies participated in both the Revolutionary War and the Civil War. But it wasn't until World War II that they became an official—and incredibly important—part of a war effort. Many heroic female

spies made a difference in World War II, often at a great personal cost. "Few men showed greater courage, bore greater responsibilities, or took greater risks,"[1] writes one historian.

World War II took a huge toll on countries around the globe. Fifty million people lost their lives, hundreds of millions more were injured, many cities were severely damaged, and countless homes were destroyed.

On June 28, 1919, just after the First World War, leaders gathered in France to sign the Treaty of Versailles. Ironically, the severe penalties on Germany imposed by the treaty inadvertently created conditions that led to another world war just two decades later.

The origins of World War II can be found in the aftermath of World War I. After World War I, the Treaty of Versailles, signed in 1919, labeled Germany as the war's aggressor, holding the country responsible for civilian damages to other European nations. Germany was then forced to pay reparations to England, France, and the other countries that had won the war. Also, according to the treaty, Germany wasn't allowed to have a large army. These restrictions made many people in Germany resent countries like England. In addition, with the worldwide economic depression of the 1930s, the German postwar economy was suffering even worse.

These factors allowed Adolf Hitler and his Nazi Party to become popular in Germany. Hitler blamed others for the depression that had a stranglehold on Germany. He promised to improve the economy and resurrect Germany as a military force. His ideas and passionate speeches sparked much of the German population. By 1933, Hitler was firmly in control in Germany, and by the late 1930s, it became clear that his ultimate goal was European domination.

Similar things were happening in Italy, where Benito Mussolini had risen to power. Likewise,

Japan was facing severe economic problems. Eventually, both Japan and Italy would join Germany in Hitler's quest for world domination.

The first part of Hitler's plan was to take over Poland, Germany's neighbor to the east. In the early morning hours of September 1, 1939, German troops poured into Poland from three directions. German airplanes bombed cities, roads,

Adolf Hitler was often referred to as the Führer (the Leader), and he believed in pan-Teutonicism—uniting all German-speaking peoples. Even his adversaries admitted that he had a great gift for exciting a crowd with his speeches. Above, Hitler salutes a crowd of followers in 1938.

and airports, quickly rendering the Polish military helpless. In just a few weeks, Germany completely controlled Poland and thousands were dead.

Many nations sprang into action when Poland was invaded. England and France declared war on Germany a few days after the invasion, and World War II officially began. Many other countries joined England and France and became known as the Allied powers. Germany, Italy, and Japan were known as the Axis powers.

The Axis attacks and invasions continued throughout 1939 and 1940, and many European countries fell to Germany. Eventually, even France was defeated. Complete control of Europe seemed to be within Hitler's grasp. By September 1940, Germany had begun bombing England. In June 1941, the Germans moved east, invading Russia.

Where was the United States? After World War I, the United States didn't want to be involved in international matters, even if it meant leaving allies like England to fight alone. But everything changed on December 7, 1941, when Japan bombed the U.S. Navy base at Pearl Harbor, Hawaii. It was now clear that the United States could remain neutral no longer. A day later, the United States declared war on the Axis powers.

The war continued to be fought on a number of fronts. While German and Italian forces battled the Allies in Europe and Russia, Japanese forces focused on dominating the Pacific in areas such as the Philippines. With Allied victories in North Africa in late 1942 and more victories in early 1943 in Russia, the war began to turn in the Allies' favor. Germany was becoming weaker, and the Allied forces had successes in Italy and France in mid-1944. By January 1945, the German army was nearly destroyed. On April 29, 1945, Hitler committed suicide. Germany officially surrendered a few days later.

Although victory was declared in Europe, the war in the Pacific continued. It wasn't until August 1945, when the United States dropped atomic bombs on Hiroshima and Nagasaki, Japan, that the war came to an end and an Allied victory was declared on August 14.

Prior to World War II, Americans didn't like the idea of using spies. After World War I, President Woodrow Wilson thought the United States could rely on its allies to provide information through their spy activities. Because of this, the United States had no formal spy agency before World War II. Almost as soon as the United States

When America entered World War II, the Office of Strategic Services (OSS) became the first centralized U.S. intelligence system. Women played an invaluable role in this operation. Above, women gather their bags at a railway station and await orders.

entered that war, however, it quickly became clear that spying would be a necessary part of the military effort. The government scrambled to set up a spy agency.

The Office of Strategic Services (OSS) was established in 1942 by President Franklin D. Roosevelt and was headed by Major General William J. "Wild Bill" Donovan, a World War I veteran. With the help and advice of the Special

Operations Executive (SOE), a British spy agency, Donovan swiftly pulled together a team of intelligent, hard-working people. Some became spies who conducted dangerous missions; others were translators, map readers, code breakers, or telephone operators. And, for the first time, women filled many of these roles.

The women who agreed to work as spies wanted to help in the war effort, regardless of the possible danger. They knew that they would have to rely on their brains, good sense, and luck to succeed in their missions and to avoid capture. But avoiding capture was not guaranteed. All women spies knew that "torture and death were the price of failure."[2] They could expect no special treatment from the enemy just because they were women.

These are the stories of some of the brave and resourceful women willing to put themselves in harm's way in order to serve their country.

VIRGINIA HALL

Nicknamed the Limping Lady of the OSS because of her artificial leg, Virginia Hall operated behind enemy lines in occupied France. For several years during World War II, Hall survived on her wits and strong will.

Hall was born to a wealthy family on April 6, 1906, in Baltimore, Maryland. She did well in school and was particularly interested in learning

languages. She was very active, loved sports, and was president of her high school class. Hall spent summers on her family farm, learning about and playing with animals. She didn't know it at the time, but this knowledge of farm animals would prove especially useful in her later work as a spy.

Hall attended Radcliffe and Barnard College, where she studied French, Italian, and German. After college, she was ready for adventure and went to study in Vienna, Austria, and later in Paris, where she became very skilled at speaking French. Returning to Washington, D.C., in 1929, she continued her studies at George Washington University but was soon itching to get back to Europe. In 1931, she began working at the U.S. Embassy in Warsaw, Poland, and would later work at embassies in Turkey and Austria.

It was in Turkey that Hall lost her leg. During a hunting trip, she accidentally shot herself in the foot. Before long her wound had become severely infected, and her leg had to be amputated just below the knee. Hall was fitted with an artificial leg and from then on walked with a limp. However, during her long career in espionage, she "expected and received no special favors or allowances because of the artificial limb."[1]

Hall continued working as a secretary at American embassies in Europe, but eventually she wanted to get a better job at the U.S. State Department. Unfortunately, the State Department didn't hire women or anyone with an amputated limb. Hall quit working for the government in 1939. She was frustrated with being stuck in an office, and even if the State Department disagreed, she didn't consider herself handicapped.

She then traveled around Europe and found herself in Paris when World War II broke out. Wanting to help the war effort, Hall began working at the French Ambulance Service. Hall believed that "after 12 years in Europe, it was her battle as well as that of her friends."[2] After it fell to Germany in June 1940, France became a dangerous place to live, and Hall was forced to go to England. There she found work at the U.S. Embassy in London.

While working at the embassy, Hall became known to the British spy agency, the SOE. It learned of her French language skills and familiarity with France. People at the SOE also believed Hall "possessed the courage, energy, self-confidence, and cool judgment [they] were looking for"[3] and decided to recruit her. Soon Hall was training for her new life as a spy. She learned how to work with weapons, how to operate radios and other communication devices, and how to organize groups that would try to resist Germany and take back France.

By August 1941, Hall was ready to be sent behind enemy lines. She would be the first SOE woman in the field. If Hall was nervous, she did not show it. She planned to pose as a reporter for the *New York Post*. The United States had not entered the war at this point, so American citizens like Hall still had the freedom to travel through France.

From her base in Lyons, France, Hall began gathering information while posing as a journalist. However, her cover as a journalist did not help her for long. With the bombing of Pearl Harbor in December 1941, the United States entered the war. As an American, Hall had become an enemy of Germany. She was now forced to operate in secret, steering clear of both French officials and Nazis occupying France.

Hall was too resourceful to let this new situation slow her. She was still able to pick up important information in bars and restaurants around Lyons. Hall was very friendly and motherly, and while she posed as a Frenchwoman, German

Nazi officers take a break at a sidewalk café in Paris in 1941 during the German occupation of France. When France surrendered to Germany in 1940, some French citizens in exile in England formed a collaboration called the Free French and played an important role in helping the Allies liberate France by 1944.

soldiers would tell her all about their military jobs and missions. Hall would quickly feed that information back to the SOE office in London.

In addition to gathering information, Hall also helped Allied pilots who had been shot down over France. She smuggled them and other Allied prisoners of war (POWs) out of France. Additionally, she set up safe houses, secret places where agents could base their operations in the underground fight against the Nazis. Hall recruited French citizens to help her and her fellow agents in the fight. Eventually, the Nazis became aware of Hall's work with the French resistance. The Nazis soon issued these orders: "The woman who limps is one of the most dangerous Allied agents in France. We must find her and destroy her."[4]

Conditions in France were becoming more dangerous by the day. In November 1942, Hall was again forced to leave the country. She found a Spanish guide to help her and a few other agents make the difficult trip across the Pyrenees Mountains into Spain. They faced cold weather and dangerous conditions, and Hall had a particularly difficult time dealing with her wooden leg. During the trip, she sent a message to the SOE office in London saying that "Cuthbert" was giving her trouble. The agent who received the message replied that she could have Cuthbert "eliminated." Little did he know, Cuthbert was Hall's nickname for her wooden leg!

Despite their precautions, Hall and others in her group were arrested at the Spanish border and sent to prison. There Hall shared a cell with a Spanish prostitute. When the prostitute was released, she smuggled out a letter from Hall and sent it to the U.S. Embassy in Barcelona, Spain. Finally, after six weeks in prison, Hall was released and went back to work, this time in Madrid, Spain.

In Madrid, Hall was once again using a job as a newspaper reporter as a cover. This time she was supposedly working for the *Chicago Times*. Her real job was to set up a new network of agents and safe houses. Hall had become so used to danger that she found Madrid boring and the job too easy. In November 1943, she reported to England for additional training. There she learned more about operating radios and how to prepare a parachute for a jump.

While she was training, she decided to begin working for the OSS. By working for an American agency, Hall could have her salary sent to her mother back in Maryland. Her mother would also get her benefits if Hall was killed in France.

Hall was given the code name Diane, and in March 1944, she was sent back into France. To make it less likely that the Germans still occupying France would detect her, she was carefully disguised. Her brown hair was dyed gray, and she wore heavy clothes to make her look plumper. She carried her radio transmitter tucked into an old, beat-up

WHAT ABOUT SPIES' FAMILIES?

For the most part, spies could tell their families very little—if anything at all—about what they were doing or where they were. Hall's mother believed that Virginia worked for a company in London. During the war, she sometimes wrote to the man she believed was Hall's boss, asking him for information about her daughter. Someone in his office wrote back to one of her letters, "From a security point of view there is little I am permitted to tell you . . . I can tell you . . . that she is doing an important and time-consuming job."[5] In another letter, Mrs. Hall was told, "Virginia is doing a spectacular . . . job. You have every reason to be proud of her."[6]

---

suitcase, and her forged papers identified her as a French citizen. She even disguised her distinctive limp by swinging her bad leg when she walked.

Hall knew she would have to avoid major cities in France because German officers were everywhere. She then set up her new operation in central France. She called on friends who had helped her during her first stay in Paris, and

Kathleen Coakley, exhibitions director of the Spy Museum in Washington, D.C., points out a wireless suitcase radio similar to that used by Virginia Hall. The museum opened in 2002 and displays many spy devices, including guns disguised as lipstick containers and cameras built into coat buttons.

within six months she had recruited and organized 300 agents to carry out missions against the Germans. She trained them, got weapons for them, and communicated with the OSS office in London.

Needing safe places to make her radio transmissions, Hall found a series of farmhouses to use as her base of operations. She had to move often to stay one step ahead of the Germans. Sometimes she stayed with French families and would set up her radio in the barn or in an attic. Between July 14 and August 14, 1944, Hall sent thirty-seven radio messages to London. She reported on where the German army was located and arranged for airdrops of food, money, radio equipment, medical supplies, and soap for the resistance fighters.

During the day, Hall worked as a milkmaid or goat herder, using skills from her childhood experience with the animals on her family's farm. These jobs allowed her to gather information as she delivered milk to local customers. She could also scout locations for the airdrops of supplies while working in the fields.

At night, Hall would go to the prearranged airdrop location and wait for the supplies. She described her life then as "different and difficult." She explained, "I spent my time looking for fields for [airdrops], bicycling up and down mountains, checking drop zones, visiting various contacts, doing my radio transmissions and then spending the nights out waiting, for the most part in vain, for deliveries."[7]

By early fall 1944, the Germans were being chased out of France by Allied forces. To help the Allies, Hall trained a new group to make things as difficult as possible for German troops remaining

French engineers purposefully demolished vital railroads and bridges as the French army retreated under the Nazi offensive. The French hoped that destroying important means of transportation would slow down and complicate the Nazis' plans for occupation.

in France. Hall's group blew up bridges, destroyed German communication lines, and captured troops whenever possible. They are credited with capturing about 500 Germans and killing 150 others. During this time, Hall also met her future husband, Paul Goillot, a fellow OSS agent who had been born in France but was raised in New York City.

Hall's work during the war was valued highly, and she was awarded the Distinguished Service

Cross, an honor that had never been given to a woman or non-military officer before. President Harry S. Truman wanted to present it to her personally, but Hall thought an award ceremony would call too much attention to her and interfere with

On January 12, 1946, President Harry S. Truman presented Major General William Donovan with an Oak Leaf Cluster, which was added to the Distinguished Service Medal he had already received. Like Hall, Donovan was decorated for his service with the OSS.

At left is an Army Distinguished Service Cross, introduced in 1918. It is awarded for extraordinary heroism in connection with military operations against an armed enemy. At right is the seal of the Central Intelligence Agency, the agency that grew out of the OSS after World War II.

her future undercover work. She sent a message from Paris saying, "No, I still have work to do here."[8] Hall eventually accepted the medal in a private ceremony at the OSS office in Washington, D.C., on September 27, 1945. Major General William "Wild Bill" Donovan, the director of the OSS, presented the medal.

After the war, Hall continued to work for the OSS. In 1947, the OSS became what we now know as the Central Intelligence Agency (CIA). Hall continued to work for the CIA in Europe until 1951, and then in Washington, D.C. She quickly advanced at the CIA, and during the Cold War she helped the United States prepare for a possible war with Russia. In 1966, Hall finally retired and lived near Baltimore until her death in 1982.

CLAIRE PHILLIPS

Many spies become involved in espionage work either to serve their country or simply for the excitement. For Claire Phillips, the spy who became known as High Pockets, there was a much more personal reason for her involvement. She hoped that her spy work might save the life of her husband.

Claire grew up in Portland, Oregon, and as a young girl she was "crazy about the theatre."[1] She

left high school to tour with a traveling entertainment show as a singer and dancer. All through her twenties, she traveled around the United States and abroad before returning to Portland. There she was briefly married and had a daughter, Dian. After her divorce, in 1941, she decided to take her young daughter with her to Manila, in the Philippines, where Claire had visited while on tour and had made friends. With World War II already raging in Europe, Claire and Dian arrived in the Philippines in September 1941, just a few months before the United States entered the war.

Soon after she arrived in Manila, Claire got a job singing in the Alcazar Club. It was there that she met a young American radio

This is a photo of Claire Phillips taken before she began her work as a spy for the United States. Claire's decision to become an entertainer when she was a young woman was unconventional, but this experience made her an effective and useful spy.

operator, Sergeant John Phillips. They fell in love and almost immediately began making plans to get married. Before they could, Japan attacked Pearl Harbor, and a day later, on December 8, 1941, the United States declared war on Japan. Soon, American citizens were no longer safe from the

Japanese troops invading Manila. Claire went to the bank and withdrew all her money, bought medicine and food, and filled her suitcases with things she and Dian would need. By the middle of December, Claire and John decided that she should take Dian into the hills outside Manila to escape bombings that had begun in the city. John's military unit was also based in the hills, so he and Claire were able see each other from time to time. Claire and John weren't sure when they might be separated, so they decided to get married on Christmas Eve, 1941. After the wedding, they were

On December 7, 1941, the Japanese attacked the American battleship fleet stationed at Pearl Harbor, Hawaii. Within a short time, five of the eight battleships were sunk or sinking, with the rest damaged. Several other ships and most Hawaii-based combat planes were also destroyed, and more than 2,400 Americans were killed.

able to spend a few hours together before John had to return to his military camp.

Days later, the small village where Phillips and her daughter were living was bombed. The mother and daughter hid with some villagers in a hole in the ground. The bombings forced them to move to a safer location. Phillips spent her days in the new village helping soldiers and villagers who had been wounded in the bombings. The bombs followed them to the new village, and they were forced to move again. This time Claire had to say good-bye to John. This latest move would take her far away from his camp, and although neither of them knew it at the time, it would be the last time they would see each other.

During the winter of 1942, Phillips and her daughter continued to hide in the hills, living with Filipino families that were hiding from the Japanese armies. They had very little to eat, living on rice, sugarcane, bananas, and occasionally some animals they were able to trap. They had to deal with snakes and rats and serious illnesses like malaria.

That winter, Phillips heard that there were American soldiers living on a nearby mountain, and she decided to go to their camp to see if one of them might be John. She made the journey to the American camp but was disappointed to see that her husband was not there. She did meet an American soldier named John Boone, who suggested that Phillips could help them by returning to Manila to gather supplies. Phillips knew it was still too dangerous for her to go back to the city because the Japanese were putting all Americans in Manila into prison camps.

While continuing to hide in the hills outside Manila, Phillips undertook her first strike against the Japanese. She heard about a place where they were storing ammunition, and she considered trying to tell John Boone where it was so he could organize troops to blow it up. But Phillips decided to take action herself, and with the help of a few boys also living in the hills, she sneaked down from their hideout and set fire to the ammunition. It soon blew up, destroying the whole supply.

After her successful mission, Phillips was ready to do more to help the war cause. However, in late spring 1942, she came down with malaria and was seriously ill for weeks. She nearly died, but she eventually recovered, only to learn that the American troops had lost some significant battles against the Japanese. American soldiers were being thrown into Japanese prison camps in

Before the Geneva Convention of 1949, which set out international humanitarian standards for the treatment of prisoners of war, many countries abused captured soldiers. Pictured above shortly after their liberation in 1945 is a group of U.S. Navy officers who had been imprisoned and starved by the Japanese.

Manila, and Phillips feared her husband would be among them. She knew she'd have to return to the city to try to find him.

At the end of June, Phillips began the dangerous trip into Manila. She traveled over land and then by boat, hidden under a pile of bananas and coconuts. She knew there was no way for her to be safe unless she concealed her identity as an American. With the help of a Spanish man who worked at the Italian Embassy, she managed to get fake identity papers that said she was Italian. When the papers were ready, she had to get them stamped and signed by a Japanese official. The official asked her to promise she would not help the enemy. "Keeping my fingers firmly crossed . . . I promised, and the papers were signed,"[2] wrote Phillips in her autobiography. This was actually an easy promise for her to keep: When the official spoke of the enemy, he was referring to America. To Phillips, however, the enemy was Japan.

With her new papers identifying her as Dorothy Fuentes, Phillips was able to move freely around Manila. Her goal was to help the American soldiers, including her husband, by sending supplies, food, and medicine to the troops being held in the Japanese camps. She also wanted to help John Boone and the soldiers hiding out in the hills. To make money, she decided to return to her job as a nightclub singer. But after a few months working at someone else's club, Phillips realized it would be much better if she had her own club. She was able to get a loan from a Chinese restaurant owner, and in October 1942, Phillips opened her own nightclub. Located near the harbor where military ships docked, the Tsubaki Club became an instant hit. Phillips made sure everyone knew this was a fancy club and only high-level Japanese military officers would be welcome there.

The decision to open her own club was a very good one. Phillips made a great deal of money, and she was able to buy food and supplies for the American prisoners. There was another important and unexpected benefit: The Japanese military men who came to the club did not worry about talking about military secrets in front of Phillips and the other entertainers at the club. Phillips quickly discovered that she was overhearing information that could be used by the American military forces.

Before she could do anything with the information she was learning, she got some bad news. Phillips met a German priest who was allowed to visit the prison camps where American soldiers were being held. She asked the priest to try to find her husband and take him some food and clothing. Two weeks later, the priest telephoned: John had died of malaria in late July in the prison camp where he had been held. Phillips was devastated by this news. All along she had believed she would be reunited with John when the war was over.

The news of John's death made Phillips more determined than ever to help the soldiers in the camps. She also made plans to get the military information she was learning at her club to John Boone. Soon after a profitable holiday season at the Tsubaki Club, Phillips sent some money to Boone along with a note that read, "Our new show a sell-out. You can count on regular backing. Standing by for orders and assignments."[3] She signed the note "High Pockets," a nickname she picked because she had begun hiding notes and money in her bra. Boone sent back a message saying that the most important thing he needed was a radio. He could use the radio to communicate with other troops hiding out in the hills. The information might even reach General Douglas MacArthur, the leader of the American troops in the Pacific.

Along with information, Phillips began sending food, clothes, shoes, and soap to Boone and the troops he had working for him. To prevent messages from being discovered, the messengers would "split the center banana in a bunch, put a message inside, and fasten the skin back into place."[4] Eventually Phillips also managed to find a radio transmitter and sent it to Boone one piece at a time. Once the radio was put together, Boone

On May 22, 1951, Claire Phillips is greeted at LaGuardia Airport in New York by Major Kenneth Boggs after being awarded the Medal of Freedom. Boggs survived cruel treatment as a POW and was eventually rescued, thanks to information provided by Phillips.

began transmitting the information Phillips had overheard at the club. Boone's messages reached General MacArthur, and he would send messages back with new instructions for Phillips. One message asked her to find out what she could about an aircraft carrier docked in the harbor in Manila. Phillips befriended the captain of the Japanese ship and was able to find out when he was leaving and where the ship was headed. When she passed this information to Boone, she knew American forces would probably destroy the ship. Because she liked the Japanese captain, "[She] even cried real tears when he left, as [she] knew [she] was sending him to his doom . . . but war is war."[5]

While gathering information that would be helpful to the Americans, Phillips also continued to send food and money to the men in the prison camps. She began working with a network of other Americans and Filipinos who were running their own operations to help the prisoners. They set up codes to signal each other. If there were letters ready to be smuggled into the camps, they would call each other and say, "Bring your recipes. I'm going to bake today."[6] They had code names for each other, and in case the Japanese were eavesdropping on their conversations, they spoke in American slang or pig latin to disguise their real plans. This could easily throw off listeners who did not speak English fluently.

The money, food, and letters reaching the men in the prison camps were well received. Phillips would sometimes get letters from prisoners, such as this one she got from a prisoner named Gentry: "I had . . . given up hope of help, even though I heard several men here talking about an angel named High Pockets sending things in."[7]

Sometimes the things she sent reached men she had known before the war. Charles Di Maio, a navy officer, had been a friend of her husband's, and when he received the package she sent him, he wrote, "Take care of yourself High Pockets. You deserve more medals than all of us in here."[8]

Phillips's operations continued to go smoothly until mid-May 1944, when members of her network were arrested one after another. Phillips knew she might be next, and friends suggested that she should hide in the hills with Boone's troops. She later wrote, "I felt that I owed it to the memory of my [husband] to remain and help his former comrades, regardless of any serious consequences to myself."[9]

On May 23, her resolve was put to the test when four Japanese police officers came to her door. They searched the rooms in her apartment and the office of the Tsubaki Club and told her she would have to go with them. Telling her young daughter that she would be home soon, Phillips was dragged away. She was thrown in a cell, blindfolded, questioned about her activities, and hit or kicked if she didn't provide the answer the Japanese officers were looking for.

Given very little food and water, covered with fleas and lice, bitten by rats, packed into cells with other prisoners, and tortured over and over again, Phillips barely survived her first few months in prison. By August, the prison guards were trying anything they could to get her to talk. One day they tied her to a bench, shoved a hose in her mouth, then turned on the water. Phillips tried to hold her breath but they punched her in the stomach and the water gushed down her throat. She passed out, but her captors woke her by putting burning cigars on her legs. Finally, one day, they told Phillips she was going to be executed. They put her in a guillotine and lowered the blade onto her neck. "This is it" thought Phillips, and then she "mercifully blacked out."[10] But it was just another attempt to get her to talk.

In late September, guards came to get Phillips. She believed she was going to be released but was instead taken to a courtroom. Forced to plead guilty to being a spy, Phillips was sentenced to death. She wasn't afraid because she "figured that death would bring a speedy end to my seemingly endless ordeal of starvation, torture, and illness."[11] However, once again, Phillips's life was spared and she was moved to a new prison and sentenced to twelve years of hard labor.

Finally, after more than eight months in captivity, Phillips was rescued by American troops on

In this scene from the film *I Was an American Spy*, actors Gene Evans and Ann Dvorak play Corporal Boone and Claire Phillips, who are hiding in the woods near Manila, waiting for the return of Philips's husband, John.

February 10, 1945. When she saw the troops, she could barely believe her eyes. She ran up to a soldier and touched his arm to make sure she wasn't imagining him. Phillips was soon reunited with her daughter, Dian, and they were finally able to return together to the United States after their long ordeal. As they sailed out of the harbor in Manila, she thought of how she had arrived four years earlier, never imagining all the things that would happen to her.

After the war, the movie *I Was an American Spy* captured Phillips's war adventures. In 1951, Claire Phillips was awarded the Medal of Freedom for her service to her country. She died in 1960 at age fifty-two.

3 ALINE GRIFFITH

Aline Griffith's exciting life took her from the world of high fashion to the danger and intrigue of espionage. Born in 1923 in Pearl River, New York, Griffith was working as a model in New York City when she was recruited by the OSS. After her adventures during World War II, Griffith married a Spanish count and went on to write several books about her many spy missions both during and after the war.

At a dinner party in September 1943, Griffith mentioned to another guest her desire to help in the war effort. She told the man that one of her brothers was a fighter pilot flying in Europe and another brother was serving on a submarine in the Pacific. She had been hoping to do something to help the United States in the war and was yearning for an adventure. The man at the party said he might be able to help her with both goals.

In this photo, circa 1938, a group of high-society fashion models gathers in a waiting room. Modeling was one of the few professions open to women at that time, and although the pay was not particularly high, it offered women glamour and the chance to travel.

Just a few weeks later, Griffith received a phone call instructing her to report to Washington, D.C. She was told to use a false name, leave her identification at home, and not tell anyone where she was going. Once in Washington, Griffith was given the code name "Tiger" and was sent for training to a location known as the Farm, in the countryside near Washington.

At the Farm, Griffith learned to crack safes and pick locks; she was taught how to make invisible ink and even how to use a folded newspaper as a weapon. Along with the other recruits—all of whom were men—she was put through endless obstacle courses, practiced hand-to-hand combat techniques, and learned to use various weapons. The future spies learned to read maps and use Morse code. They also went on practice missions where they were assigned to follow people and avoid being followed themselves. Griffith and her fellow recruits worked for twenty-one days straight before they got their first day off.

After her grueling training, Griffith's first assignment was in Spain. To prepare, she studied the history, politics, and geography of Spain. She learned that although Spain was officially neutral, many U.S. officials suspected that the country was helping Hitler. The OSS believed that someone in Madrid was giving Allied information to Germany. The OSS had a list of four suspects, and it wanted Griffith to find out which one was the traitor.

Operation Bullfight, as Griffith's mission was known, began with a flight to Spain. Griffith had told friends and family that she was going to Spain to work at the American Oil Mission, a real company that was being used as a cover for OSS spies in Madrid. Soon after Griffith arrived, she witnessed a man being murdered in a casino. When she discovered that the man was a fellow agent, she knew her mission was for real. It would be as dangerous as it was important.

Once she reported to work at the American Oil Mission, she learned that her boss there was actually a fellow agent. At their first meeting, he explained Operation Bullfight, which involved getting information to help the Allies with their planned invasion of Germany from the south. Their other mission was to find the double agent working for Germany. After he finished, he cautioned her, saying, "Miss Griffith, if you do not follow orders strictly, you could be responsible for hundreds—or thousands—of deaths of American soldiers."[1]

Every day, Griffith reported to work, supposedly for the American Oil Mission. Instead, during the day she was reading coded secret messages from all over the world. After work, she had a second and perhaps more important job. She was assigned to attend parties and get to know people in Madrid. The OSS thought Griffith would be able to get information from these people without them ever suspecting she was a spy.

Griffith was very successful at this second part of her job. She befriended many important people in Madrid. Because of her charming personality, Griffith was able to put them at ease and get them to tell her things they may have thought were insignificant. To Griffith, these were important pieces of the puzzle she was putting together.

To help her gather information, Griffith recruited a network of Spanish women. She began her chain of informants with the woman who was helping her improve her Spanish. This woman recruited another woman, who found one more. Eventually, there were fifteen links in this chain of information. Each woman would know only the woman who hired her and the woman she hired; this would protect the whole chain. These women carried messages and gathered information helpful to the Allies. One woman paid a high price for her work with Griffith's network: She was shot to death while sleeping in Griffith's bed while Griffith was away for the weekend. Upon discovering the dead woman when she returned, Griffith realized she was the real target of the bullet. She knew that whoever murdered the woman might come back for her.

Things were getting more dangerous in Madrid. In addition to the murder of Griffith's informant, several agents were murdered. There was also an attempted assassination of Francisco Franco, the leader of Spain, at a bullfight. With the situation in Spain reaching a boiling point, her superiors gave Griffith a pill called an "L pill." The pill was loaded with poison and would kill her instantly if she

Generalísimo Francisco Franco was the head of state in Spain from 1939 until his death in 1975. Known as el Caudillo (the Leader), he presided over the authoritarian government of the Spanish state, which had overthrown the Second Spanish Republic. At left, Franco addresses a gathering of youth organizations in 1939.

bit it. She would have to use it if captured so that she could avoid being tortured into giving up secret information.

Griffith had another close call on her next major mission. She was instructed to pretend to be on a sightseeing trip to Málaga, a city on the southern coast of Spain. Griffith would carry a briefcase containing microfilm, a gun, and a radio transmitter. The real purpose of her trip was to pass the supplies to an agent who had recently arrived in Spain. On the train to Málaga, the conductor questioned her because she didn't have the right identification papers. He took her directly to jail in Málaga, and she was held there for more than twenty-four hours. The hours passed slowly as she missed her first planned meeting with her fellow agent, and then the second. She was still in jail that night, and "it seemed like the longest night of [her] life."[2] When she was finally released from jail, she hurried to the small church where she was to meet the agent and just made her third—and last— chance to deliver the important briefcase.

While Griffith continued to do her OSS work from her base at the American Oil Mission, she continued to attend parties and events around Madrid. She became close with important government connections in Spain and other European countries. At the same time, none of her friends knew that she was a spy. Coincidentally, the father of one of her friends was a German prince living in Madrid. Prince Lilienthal, who was not in favor of Nazi aggression, had important information that he wanted to pass to the Americans, and he suspected Griffith might be able to help. The prince told Griffith that he believed someone in her office was spying for the Germans. Griffith didn't know who the double agent might be, and of course she could not discuss it with anyone in her office. After all,

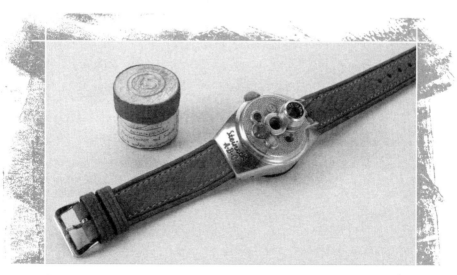

This Steineck ABC wristwatch camera, made in 1949, allowed spies to take pictures without calling attention to themselves. It had six exposures and used specially modified 35mm film. It was invented by Doctor R. Steiner, who was known for inventing a number of other espionage devices.

any one of her coworkers could be the double agent. She contacted her "handler" in Washington, who told her to keep her eyes and ears open. Griffith did just that, but she was in for more danger.

While on her way home from a party one night, the man hired to drive her home turned down an unfamiliar road. Before the car got too far, she was able to get out and duck into a nearby forest. She could hear the driver following her through the undergrowth, but she was prepared for him. In her autobiography, she describes what happened next: "I . . . crouched and shot at the shadowy form rushing at me . . . I must have missed, because he lunged for me and grabbed my throat. He was strangling me! Using my last bit of strength, I shoved the gun at him, not knowing or caring where I was aiming this time."[3] Her attacker's dead body landed on top of her, but she managed to free herself. After searching him, she ran back to the car and drove back to the city, happy to be alive.

Eventually, Griffith and her fellow agents were able to uncover the identity of the double agent working for the OSS. Once the agent was identified, Griffith and her colleagues developed a plan for her to give him incorrect information about Allied military plans. This false information threw the Germans off track, and they were unprepared for an Allied invasion of Saint Tropez, France. As a result, the invasion proceeded smoothly and was successful.

Griffith continued to work for the OSS in Spain until the end of World War II. After the war, she did some more espionage work in France and Switzerland until retiring from the OSS in 1947. The next year, she married a Spanish count in Madrid and became Aline, Countess of Romanones. She has written three books about her experiences as a spy during World War II and her further espionage missions in the 1960s and 1970s. She continues to live in Spain.

ELIZABETH "BETTY" PACK

4

By the time she was eleven years old, Amy Elizabeth Thorpe had written two books, had already lived in several states, and had even lived in Cuba. As she grew up, her adventures continued, and her life as a spy during World War II took her even farther abroad and deeper into adventure.

From the time she was born in Minneapolis, Minnesota, in 1910, Amy Elizabeth Thorpe was on

the go. Her father was a captain in the United States Marines, and his job took him to Cuba, Hawaii, Maine, Rhode Island, and Washington, D.C. Known to her family as Elizabeth (although she was later called Betty), she spent much of her time alone, observing the people and places she visited. She also enjoyed writing about things she had experienced, penning two books, the second of which her father had printed and illustrated.

Elizabeth was also constantly looking for excitement. She told one of her biographers that she sought "any kind of excitement—even fear."[1] When her father retired in 1923, the family traveled throughout Europe. There, Elizabeth learned to speak French, and she loved the adventure of travel. When her family returned to Washington, D.C., the following year, she missed Europe greatly.

When she was nineteen, Elizabeth met Arthur Pack, a much older British diplomat. A few months later, in April 1930, they were married. In the early years of their marriage, the couple lived in New York, Chile, England, and Spain. While they were living in Spain in 1936, the Spanish Civil War was raging. It is suspected that Elizabeth Pack may have begun her work as a spy for the British government during this time. She helped

This Spanish Civil War Republican propaganda poster, circa 1938, reads "Defending Madrid is Defending Catalonia." The Spanish Republican forces were defeated by Axis-supported forces in 1938. Both Madrid and the region of Catalonia were captured.

some soldiers trapped in enemy territory by smuggling them over the border. She loved the danger and excitement of the situation and felt that "she had found her true calling at last."[2]

Arthur was transferred to Warsaw, Poland, in 1937. Some historians suspect that he was transferred so that the British Secret Intelligence Service (SIS) could use Elizabeth Pack in Poland. In the winter of 1938, Arthur had a stroke and returned to England to recover. Meanwhile, Pack began an affair with a Polish diplomat, Edward Kulikowski. He told her about Hitler's plans to take over Czechoslovakia. Pack knew this information would be of great importance, and she passed it to her friend Jack Shelley. As she suspected, he and the British government were very interested in her information and formally recruited her to work for the SIS in March 1938. SIS officials in London were pleased to have Pack working for them. They asked her to gather as much information as possible by befriending Polish officials.

One of the first important men she met was Count Michal Lubienski. He had access to government documents, and she knew he would have top-secret information on Poland's dealings with Germany. Pack began an affair with him, and it is believed that one of the most important things she learned about was the Enigma machine.

The Enigma was a code machine that was being used by the Germans. The Enigma was similar to a typewriter but had a complicated system of gears that produced codes impossible to break unless you knew how the gears had been configured when the code was originally written. The SIS suspected that Poland might know how to break the Enigma code, and they hoped Pack could get information from Lubienski. Pack was able to find out where Polish research on the Enigma was being done, and she confirmed that the Poles were reading Enigma messages. The full extent of her help isn't known for sure because the existence of the Enigma was not even revealed until the 1970s.

Perhaps one of the most crucial inventions of World War II, the Enigma machine helped the Allies decode encrypted German messages. It is widely believed that if the Allies had not cracked the Enigma's codes, World War II would have lasted well into 1946.

With the prospect of war looming, Pack was forced to leave Warsaw in 1938 and return to London. Meanwhile, Arthur had recovered from his stroke, and he and Pack were sent to Czechoslovakia and then to Chile. From there, Pack tried to keep up with what was happening in Poland. She was very worried about the war and missed being involved. When Germany invaded Poland in September 1939, it was even harder for

ENIGMA'S ENORMOUS PUZZLE

The Enigma machine could produce 150 quintillion (150,000,000,000,000,000,000) combinations of numbers. It is no surprise that it was nearly impossible to break the codes it produced. In 1939, the British assembled a team of 100 code breakers at Bletchley Park, 5 miles (8 kilometers) north of London. Soon there were 10,000 code breakers working there, many of them women. Eventually, with the help of codebooks discovered on a captured German submarine, the team was able to break the code and read the German Enigma codes. Having the codes allowed the Allies to anticipate the Germans' plans.

Pack not to be helping, and she frequently wrote to the SIS to get more work as an agent. She volunteered to return to Europe, even though the war was raging. Finally, in June 1940, the War Office in London wrote to tell her they could use her help. Leaving her husband behind, she sailed for London in early July and began working right away. There were political leaders from Chile on the boat with her, and they provided some valuable information. However, her mission was cut short when her ship arrived in Lisbon, Portugal. There she got a telegram from Arthur telling her he needed her in Chile. Disappointed, she began the long trip back by boat. While on the boat, she met Paul Fairly, an American who worked for the Office of Naval Intelligence. He told Pack she might be able to help them with spy work. At this point, "she had reached a point where she was not prepared to allow anything to stand in the way of her participation in the fight [against Hitler]."[3]

Finally, in early 1941, Peck was able to return to the excitement of spy work. She sailed from Chile to New York City, where she was met by Fairly. He gave her a coded letter with a phone number for her to call. Calling the number, she reached John Arthur Reed Pepper. He became her handler for her work with the British Security Coordination (BSC). America was not yet involved in the war, and the BSC was a little worried that Pack would have trouble working for the British. They asked her if "she felt strongly enough [about ending the war] to work for us in your own country, [to] spy on your fellow Americans and report to us."[4] They warned her to beware of the FBI and further warned her, "[I]f you are caught, we haven't heard of you. You understand that?"[5]

Pack assured the BSC that she could handle the job. She set up house in Washington, D.C., and began throwing parties for politicians and diplomats stationed in Washington. Working under the code name Cynthia, Pack completed several assignments for the BSC.

In the spring of 1941, Pack was given a mission that would change her life. Her superiors encouraged her to get to know Charles Brousse, a French diplomat living in Washington. By this time, France was under the control of the Germans. However, the United States still maintained contact with the Vichy government—the government of the small part of France not controlled by Germany. The British hoped they could prevent the Vichy government from falling to the Germans. They also hoped to gain valuable information about German plans from French officials.

Pack followed orders and quickly got to know Brousse. Soon they had fallen in love, which did not prevent her from passing any information she got from him to her bosses. Eventually, Brousse began providing information

French diplomat Charles Brousse visits Washington, D.C., with Betty Pack. The two worked together to steal codebooks that would enable the Allies to intercept and interpret German messages.

directly to the BSC. In the spring of 1942, Pack was given her most difficult assignment yet. She was asked to steal the French navy's secret codes (called ciphers) stored in a safe in the French Embassy. These codes would help the Allies decipher secret messages and find out what the French and German plans were well ahead of time. Brousse decided to risk his career to help his lover.

Around the same time, Pack began reporting to the OSS, the new American spy agency. She was given a new contact in Washington and plans got under way. Pack was worried about this new assignment. She wrote in her diary, "I was apprehensive about what I had promised. I worried that I had led my chiefs into placing too much confidence in my capabilities."[6] Nevertheless, she spent the next several months devising a plan to steal the codebooks.

After several months, Pack, her contacts at the OSS, and Brousse finally came up with a plan, and they were ready to put it into action on the night of June 19, 1942. Pack and Brousse had befriended the night watchman at the French Embassy, and he was not surprised to see them there that night. Pack and Brousse invited him to share some champagne with them. They had slipped a knockout drug into his drink, and he quickly fell asleep. As soon as the watchman was asleep, Pack let in a man known as the Georgia Cracker. He was a safe cracker whom the OSS had had released from prison to do this job, and they felt confident he would be able to pick the lock on the door of the room where the safe was located, as well as the safe itself. However, cracking the safe turned out to be not quite as easy as planned. The early morning hours dragged on with no progress on the safe. By the time they cracked the code to the safe, it was nearly 4:00 AM, the deadline for when they had to be out of the embassy to avoid being discovered. Tired and disappointed, they had to leave the books in the safe and begin planning another attempt.

The next day, Pack was able to convince the OSS that the team should try again the next night. The only problem was that the Georgia Cracker was not available. The OSS wondered if she would be willing to try again, using the combination they had learned from the first attempt. Brousse was worried about this plan, but Pack was eager to put the plan in motion. The following night, avoiding the guard whom they could not risk drugging again, Pack picked the lock on the door to the room with the safe. She quickly went to work on the safe, using the combination she had memorized, "but it would not budge. She tried over and over for what seemed like hours but she could not open the door."[7] It was getting late, so, once again, Pack had to abandon the mission. At about 3:00 AM, she reported to her OSS contact, who told her to fly to New York the following morning.

When she arrived in New York, she was taken to a beach on Long Island. There, a van was waiting—with the Georgia Cracker and a safe inside. He spent three hours teaching her how to open the safe, similar to the one in the embassy. He taught her to open it by feel, and Pack was successful at last. However, she was worried that she would not be able to open the real safe, so arrangements were made for the Georgia Cracker to join her on the next attempt.

Finally, the third time the dangerous plan was put into action, the team was successful. The safe was opened quickly and easily, and the Georgia Cracker slipped out a window with the codebooks. He took them to a nearby hotel room, where a team of photographers waited to take a picture of each page. Pack and Brousse remained in the embassy, worrying the whole time about what would happen if the books did not return on time.

The Georgia Cracker did return with the codebooks, although he was almost forty minutes late. They put the books back in the safe, cleaned up the room, and went to the hotel room where the books had been photographed. According to Mary Lovell, "It seemed as though the entire [room] was filled with tables and photographic equipment, lights, cameras, tripods, cables, and people. But most

General George Patton *(left)* and Dwight D. Eisenhower make plans for the invasion of North Africa, called Operation Torch. The United States expected the Vichy-controlled areas of Africa not to fight. The United States wanted the area so it could attack Germany from the south. However, Hitler forced Vichy's leaders to fight the Allied offensive, and many French were killed by Allied forces as a result. Pack's espionage work greatly contributed to the Allied victory.

important were the photographs of the ciphers spread around the room, apparently to dry, on the tables, on the furniture, on the floor."[8] When Pack saw the pictures of the codes, she realized the important job she had just accomplished. Montgomery Hyde writes, "[I]t was the proudest moment of her life."[9]

Pack and Brousse were congratulated for their completion of the important mission. The photos of the codebooks were flown to England within a day and are said to have saved 100,000 lives. There is no way to verify that number, but having the codes certainly helped the Allies. Operation Torch, an Allied invasion of North Africa on November 8, 1942, was aided by the fact that the Allies had the French codes.

Colonel Ellery Huntington of the OSS told Pack a few days after the attack that the mission had been a huge success and that it was due to her ciphers. He said, "They have changed the whole course of the war."[10]

Although this was Pack's most successful mission, it also proved to be her last. The OSS considered sending her to London for more training, but a new plan was developed to send her to France with Brousse.

A British ship is engulfed in flames after being struck by the French or German forces defending Casablanca during Operation Torch. Although the Allies took some heavy damage, by 1943 North Africa was in Allied hands.

Due to several complications, she and Brousse did not sail to France until October 1944, and by then the war was nearly over.

Pack lived the rest of her life in France. She and Brousse divorced their spouses and married, living in a French castle. Pack began writing her memoirs, but she died of cancer in 1963, before she finished writing the story of her life. She didn't think anyone would find her life interesting, but her adventures are still remembered today.

JOSEPHINE BAKER

Not all female spies were unknown women working in the shadows. Some were already famous and made good spies because of their celebrity. Josephine Baker, the famous singer and dancer, did her part in World War II by carrying secret messages in plain sight.

Baker was born into a poor family in St. Louis, Missouri, in 1906. She got her first job when she

In this photo, circa 1925, Josephine Baker strikes a pose in a silk evening dress and diamond earrings. Baker began her career in New York performing in Harlem's Plantation Club. She was commonly referred to as the Black Venus.

was just eight years old and worked hard all through her childhood, helping to support her family. By the time she was thirteen, she had found her true calling: dance. She practiced as much as she could and dreamed of one day doing an act onstage. At about the same time, she had a fight with her mother and decided to move out of the house. She worked as a waitress and got married when she was just fourteen. The marriage didn't last long, and she went back to waitressing until she got the chance to join a group called the Jones Family Band as a dancer and trombone player. She toured with various groups for the next several years and had another brief marriage. Her big break came in 1925 when she went to Paris with a dance group. She was a huge hit in France as well as other European countries.

Baker spent the rest of the 1920s touring in Europe before returning to Paris in 1930, where she starred in another show and led a glamorous life. She even had a pet leopard that would walk down the street or take taxis with her. Baker was married again briefly in 1937 and continued to live the life of a star. Then war broke out.

When France declared war on Germany in September 1939, Baker was eager to get involved in the war effort. She was not sure how she could help, but the brother of her agent had an idea. He contacted Jacques Abtey, a spy who worked for the French military and was recruiting civilians to help with the war. Abtey wasn't sure Baker would make an ideal spy. He remembered the story of Mata Hari, a famous dancer and spy who had been executed during World War I for spying for the Germans. When he met Baker, Abtey changed his

Mata Hari, a famous turn-of-the-century dancer, had many lovers and male confidants who were involved in politics. In 1917, she was put on trial in France and was accused of spying as a double agent for Germany and France in World War I. She was found guilty and was executed by firing squad on October 15, 1917.

mind. Baker convinced him that she was very loyal to France and wanted to do anything she could to help. As a star, Baker had befriended many rich and powerful people in France, people who wouldn't mind telling her things. In fact, in the early days of her spy career, she was so sure she would not be suspected that she wrote information she had obtained on her arms and hands. When

JULIA CHILD: SPY

Long before she became a world-famous chef, Julia Child worked as a secret agent for the OSS. She worked on special projects like developing a repellent that would protect mines planted in the ocean from being eaten—and detonated—by sharks before the mines could blow up the German submarines they were intended for. Later in the war, Child ran the code rooms in India and China, organizing and filing top-secret messages coming in from all over the world. After the war, Child was recognized for her work with an award called the Emblem for Civilian Service.

---

warned that it was a dangerous thing to do, she replied, "Oh, nobody would think I'm a spy."[1]

At first, Abtey's fellow spies worried that Baker might not be strong enough for spy work, but Abtey convinced them she was as strong as steel. With her first few missions, she impressed them by being cool in tough situations. She was also endlessly optimistic, assuring them that America would enter the war and the Allies would be sure to win.

Josephine Baker *(right)* cracks a smile during her service as a volunteer in the Free French Women's Air Auxiliary. After her death in 1975, Baker became the first American woman to receive French military honors at her funeral.

From September 1939 to May 1940, Baker gathered information at parties, giving anything she thought might be important to Abtey. During the day, Baker helped people coming to Paris from Belgium in an attempt to escape Hitler.

When the Germans took over France in June 1940, black people were no longer safe from Hitler, especially in Paris. Even a famous enter-tainer like Baker could be arrested or killed by

Nazis. Baker decided to go to her home in the south of France where the Germans were not yet in control. Abtey eventually joined her there to await their orders for a secret mission.

When their orders came through, Abtey and Baker learned they would be traveling to Portugal to deliver information to an agent there. Before they left, they needed to get the necessary permits and visas that would allow them to travel. For Baker this was easy. Everyone knew her and it was easy to pretend that she was traveling to Portugal to perform. It was not as easy for Abtey, but he managed to get a fake passport and they were ready to go. All that was left was to figure out how to get the information across the border. They decided to write it in invisible ink on Baker's sheet music so that they would not need to hide it. In November 1940, they headed to Spain by train and crossed the border easily. No one suspected Baker, and no one even looked at Abtey—they were too busy looking at Baker. Once in Portugal, they took a plane to Lisbon, where Abtey was able to pass the information to his contact there.

Baker and Abtey lived in Algiers in North Africa while awaiting their next assignment. This time Abtey had trouble getting the paperwork that would allow him to travel. Baker was forced to go alone. Again she wrote the information in invisible ink on her sheet music. "[W]ho would have guessed it was covered with invisible notations about the [location of the Germans] in southwest France?"[2] she later wrote. She crossed the ocean to Portugal and delivered the information. While she was there, she performed in some shows, went to parties, and gathered more information before returning to Algiers.

Spain was the next stop for Baker. Throughout the spring of 1941, she traveled to major cities in Spain, performing and gathering information along the way. There were many German military officers in Spain, and they were more than happy to talk to the famous and charming Baker. "Being Josephine Baker had definite advantages. Wherever I went I was swamped with invitations,"[3] she wrote in her autobiography. She managed to get a great deal of helpful information. At the end of the night, "I carefully recorded everything I'd heard. My notes would be highly compromising had they been discovered, but who would dare search Josephine Baker to the skin? The information remained snugly in place, secured [to her underwear] by a safety pin."[4]

Despite all her success, her career as a spy was about to end. In June 1941, she was hospitalized for a severe infection. She remained in the hospital until December 1942 and was so ill that at one point American newspapers reported that she had died. While in the hospital, Baker was not entirely out of the espionage business. Abtey was able to pass information to American military and government officials visiting Baker in the hospital.

Once Baker was finally out of the hospital, she decided to help the war effort in another way. Throughout the rest of the war she performed for Allied troops, trying to boost the morale of the soldiers. The American military officials were happy to have her. In fact, in May 1944, the chief of the air force general staff issued an order to all military officials that they were to use military planes and trucks to help Baker get to her performances.

After the war, Baker's work was recognized by France, who gave her the Medal of Resistance in October 1946. She missed the excitement of the war but married again, adopted twelve children, and traveled and performed all over the world. In the 1950s, she returned to the United States, fighting for civil rights for African Americans. She spoke in front of 200,000 people at the March on

Josehphine Baker *(left)* and some of her adopted children pose for a family photo in 1959. Unable to have children of her own, Baker ultimately adopted twelve orphans, whom she called her Rainbow Tribe.

Washington on August 28, 1963, alongside Martin Luther King Jr.

Baker suffered a heart attack in 1973, and after nearly fifty years of performing, she began to slow down. On April 8, 1975, she gave her final performance. Two days later, she died of a stroke.

MARY BANCROFT

Like several other women who grew up to be spies, as a child Mary Bancroft was eager for excitement and adventure, and she wanted to grow up quickly. When Bancroft was an adult, she found her childhood journals and saw that when she was nine she had written, "I am *almost* an adult." At twelve, she noted, "I am now an adult, but nobody seems to realize it."[1] Born in Boston,

Massachusetts, on October 29, 1903, Mary Bancroft was a curious and adventurous child. Her family was wealthy, and she was very close to the father of her stepmother, C. W. Barron. He was the publisher of the *Wall Street Journal*, and he encouraged her adventurous spirit and suggested she become a journalist.

As a teenager, Bancroft's father took her to New York City to watch a World War I victory parade in April 1919. As she watched the soldiers pass by, she was both excited and depressed. She wrote, "[I] longed for a life of adventure. I wanted to go everywhere, see everything."[2] But she thought nothing exciting would ever happen to her. In her autobiography, she writes, "[I was] terribly disappointed when I learned that, because I was a girl, I couldn't fulfill my most cherished ambition of becoming a cop. I probably couldn't even be a glamorous spy like Mata Hari, whom the French had shot. There was nothing glamorous about me."[3] Things would turn out much differently for Bancroft than she believed at the time.

Bancroft went to Smith College, but immediately after her first year she married Sherwin Badger, and they went to live in Cuba for a year. When they returned to the United States, the couple lived in

In 1919, elated that the First World War had finally ended, thousands of Americans gathered in the streets to show their appreciation for their troops. Bancroft and her father attended this welcome home parade in New York City.

Boston and then in New York City, where Bancroft wrote some articles for her grandfather's publications, the *Wall Street Journal* and *Barron's*. Bancroft and Badger had two children together, but eventually they divorced when the children were still very young. Soon after her divorce, Bancroft took a boat to Europe, and on her trip met Jean Rufenacht, a Swiss businessman. They married, and Bancroft went to live with him in Zurich, Switzerland.

While living in Zurich during the 1930s, Bancroft watched the beginnings of World War II closely. In 1934, she visited Germany and was scared by what she saw there. Hitler's grip on Germany was growing stronger, and she wasn't sure what would happen. Bancroft was listening to the radio, along with the rest of Europe, as Hitler invaded Czechoslovakia in 1938. She was listening again as England declared war on Germany in September 1939 and continued to listen as country after country was invaded by the Germans.

During the first years of the war, Bancroft and her family were just trying to get by in Switzerland, dealing with shortages of food and heating oil. Soon Switzerland was completely surrounded by countries that were controlled by the Germans. Although she worried about what might

Despite the dangers of their life during the war, OSS members would still manage to get together with friends for a relaxing evening. At left, Allen Dulles and Mary Bancroft sit with friends in a café in Bern, Switzerland, during World War II. Switzerland's neutrality during the war made it a haven for those fleeing the Nazis.

happen to her and her family, she wanted to stay in her adopted country. However, she was also eager to help the United States with the war effort, even if she was not living there. Bancroft was not sure how she could help, but when a man from the United States Embassy called to ask if she would write articles about the war for Swiss and American newspapers, she jumped at the chance to play even a small role.

What Bancroft did not know was that the man who had contacted her was really recruiting her to work for the OSS. In December 1942, he introduced her to Allen Dulles, an American man working at the U.S. Embassy. At first Bancroft was not aware of who Dulles was, but she soon discovered that he was working on intelligence missions for the OSS.

By January 1943, Bancroft was carrying out small missions for the OSS, working closely with Dulles. Bancroft's work as a journalist provided a good cover for her spy work. She was able to meet lots of people, go to parties, and travel freely. At the end of every week, she would take the train to Bern, Switzerland, where Dulles was based. There, she would turn over information she had gathered that week. Dulles and Bancroft would call intelligence officials in Washington, D.C., and issue their report. They knew that the Swiss officials might be listening in on these phone calls so Bancroft would sometimes slip in false information to throw them off track.

Bancroft was successful in her information-gathering duties. She was fluent in both German and French and was able to blend in well with Swiss citizens. Bancroft was also a good listener—a skill that helped her in her journalism *and* spying duties. She later wrote that she "very quickly learned the value of personal relationships, how important it was to win people's trust and confidence."[4] She knew that developing good sources of information was extremely important. Those initial sources could lead her to their sources and so on. Bancroft described intelligence work as being like a puzzle, where you must fit all the pieces together. Small pieces of information that might seem to be insignificant could turn out to bring the whole picture into focus.

After they had worked together a few months, Dulles told Bancroft that he had a much more important project for her. A German military man named Hans Gisevius had been in contact with Dulles and was interested in turning over military information to the Allies. Gisevius worked for the Abwehr, part of the German military. However, Gisevius didn't like the Nazis—not because what they were doing was wrong, but because he thought he was better than them. He had been sent to Switzerland to make contact with the Allies and begin making plans to overthrow Hitler.

Gisevius also wanted Dulles to help him translate into English a book he had written about the Nazis. He wanted to be able to publish it in America as soon as the war was over. Dulles agreed to help Gisevius—and help the OSS while he was at it. Dulles's plan was to have Bancroft do the translation and get any information she could from Gisevius while she was working with him. Dulles told Bancroft, "I want you to report to

Hans Gisevius, shown here testifying at the Nuremburg trials in 1946, felt concern over what the Nazi Party was doing to Germany even before war broke out. The trials were held to punish Nazi leaders for war crimes committed during World War II.

me everything he says to you—everything. With you working on his book, he may be off his guard and say things to you that contradict the story he is telling me."[5] Bancroft was nervous about the new job and afraid that she would not be able to handle this large task.

At their first meeting, Bancroft was surprised to see that Gisevius had brought 1,415 pages of manuscript—and that wasn't even the whole book! Bancroft knew she had to be careful with Gisevius. She thought he might be spying on her so she could not reveal anything that would be helpful to him. At the same time, she had to gain his trust so that he might tell her things he wouldn't tell Dulles. She also had to keep him happy so that he would continue to help the OSS.

Early in July 1944, Gisevius disappeared suddenly. Bancroft believed he had gone to Germany, but she was not sure what he was doing there. That month Bancroft went on vacation, taking Gisevius's manuscript with her. On July 20, Bancroft learned of a failed attempt to kill Hitler. But it was not until she returned to Zurich in September that she learned what had happened to Gisevius. Gisevius had been involved in the plot to assassinate Hitler, and she was unsure whether he was alive or dead. Bancroft finally heard from him in January 1945, but "he looked at least ten years older. His hair had turned gray and he had lost a tremendous amount of weight."[6] At first Gisevius was too tired to talk, but after a few days his story came pouring out. He and his group had planted a bomb that had gone off but had not killed Hitler. Many other conspirators had been captured and

In 1944, Adolf Hitler *(right)* and Benito Mussolini inspect the wreckage of the conference room at Hitler's headquarters after a failed assassination attempt. Hitler survived the bombing because he was shielded from the blast by a conference table. Although four people were killed, Hitler was only slightly injured. The plot ringleaders were caught that night and executed on July 21.

executed, but Gisevius had escaped, using a fake passport Dulles had arranged to have made and sent to him in Germany.

When the war in Europe was finally over, Bancroft traveled on various assignments to European countries devastated by the war. In France, she got to see firsthand the destruction of cities, the graves of soldiers, and the people who still didn't have enough food, clothing, or other

COVER AND DOCUMENTATION (C&D)

A special branch of the OSS, called Cover and Documentation (C&D), helped supply spies with essential tools they would need in their work: fake passports and clothing. Both had to be completely realistic or officials might realize they were dealing with impostors. C&D used German typewriters and ink to create the passports. They found or created clothes and uniforms that looked just like the real thing. The smallest details, such as pens, wallets, and watches, had to look authentic. Even buttons had to be sewn on to uniforms in the European style.

necessities. Many people looked stunned, even though the real horrors of war were behind them.

Bancroft also went to Nuremberg, Germany, where Nazi leaders were put on trial for their war crimes. She was very interested to see the people she'd written about in the Swiss papers convicted of the horrible things they'd done.

Nazi leaders listen to the testimony against them on September 21, 1946. In the back row *(from left to right)* are Baldur von Schirach *(standing)*, Fritz Sauckel *(behind Schirach)*, Alfred Jodl, Franz von Papen, Arthur Seyss-Inquart, Albert Speer, Konstantin von Neurath, and Hans Fritzsche. In the front row are Hermann Goering, Rudolf Hess, Joachim von Ribbentrop, Wilhelm Keitel, Ernst Kaltenbrunner, Alfred Rosenberg, Hans Frank, Wilhelm Frick, Julius Streicher, Walter Funk, and Hjalmar Schacht.

Bancroft returned to the United States in 1953. She lived in New York City and kept in touch with Dulles and Gisevius. Later, Gisevius published *To the Bitter End*, the book that Bancroft had worked so hard to translate.

Bancroft never forgot her war experiences. "World War II . . . changed me, my life, my whole outlook on the world. I have never been able to see anything in the same way since."[7] When Bancroft died in January 1997, the *New York Times* recognized her for her "brilliant work in Switzerland in World War II."[8]

CONCLUSION

The stories of the brave women in this book are just a few of the many tales that could be told. Because spies work undercover, many of their exciting stories are never known. Linda McCarthy writes, "Intelligence professional[s] . . . do their duty quietly, many times putting themselves in great peril while carrying out their assigned missions . . . [T]hey shun the limelight even after many years into retirement."[1]

Being a spy can sometimes seem glamorous, but the reality—as you have seen in the stories of the women in this book—is that it is more often very hard work that is occasionally exciting but very often dangerous and sometimes even dull.

In the years since World War II, women have continued to work as spies for the U.S. government. At the CIA, the official U.S. spy agency, women hold all kinds of jobs, many serving in high-level

positions. Although the tools, such as computers and high-tech gadgets, have changed, some things haven't: the bravery, intelligence, and spirit of these women have been invaluable to the United States.

This picture, taken in 1990, shows the CIA headquarters in Langley, Virginia. Even in peacetime, it is the CIA's job to monitor potential dangers to the United States through espionage and intelligence-gathering. The CIA employs many female agents, who take their share of the hardships and danger of being a spy.

TIMELINE

October 29, 1903	Mary Bancroft is born in Boston, Massachusetts.
April 6, 1906	Virginia Hall is born in Baltimore, Maryland.
1906	Josephine Baker is born in St. Louis, Missouri.
1908	Claire Phillips is born in Portland, Oregon.
1910	Elizabeth "Betty" Pack is born in Minneapolis, Minnesota.
1923	Aline Griffith is born in Pearl River, New York.
1933	Hitler comes to power in Germany.
March 1938	Betty Pack begins working for British SIS in Poland.
September 1939	Josephine Baker begins working for French military intelligence.
September 1, 1939	Germany invades Poland.
September 3, 1939	England and France declare war on Germany.
June 14, 1941	France falls to Germany.
August 1941	Virginia Hall is recruited by the SOE and is sent to France.
September 1941	Claire Phillips arrives in Manila, Philippines.
December 7, 1941	Japan bombs Pearl Harbor, Hawaii.
December 8, 1941	United States declares war on Axis powers.
1942	Betty Pack begins working for the OSS in Washington, D.C.

June 1942	Betty Pack steals French naval ciphers from French Embassy.
October 1942	Claire Phillips opens the Tsubaki Club and begins her spy operations.
December 1942	Mary Bancroft is recruited by the OSS in Switzerland.
1943	Aline Griffith is recruited by the OSS and is sent to Spain.
May 23, 1944	Claire Phillips is arrested for spying.
July 20, 1944	German military fails in attempt to assassinate Hitler.
February 10, 1945	Claire Phillips is rescued from prison by American troops.
April 29, 1945	Hitler commits suicide.
May 7, 1945	Germany surrenders.
May 8, 1945	Victory in Europe is declared by the Allies.
August 6, 1945	United States drops atomic bomb on Hiroshima, Japan.
August 9, 1945	United States drops atomic bomb on Nagasaki, Japan.
August 14, 1945	Victory in the Pacific is declared by the Allies.
1947	The OSS becomes the CIA. Aline Griffith retires from the OSS.
1960	Claire Phillips dies.
1963	Betty Pack dies in France.
1975	Josephine Baker dies in France.
1982	Virginia Hall dies near Baltimore, Maryland.
1997	Mary Bancroft dies in New York.

Glossary

amputate To surgically remove a limb.

assassination A murder, sometimes carried out for political reasons.

cipher A message in code.

Cold War A long standoff between the United States and the U.S.S.R. over nuclear weapons.

compromise To reveal to an unauthorized person or an enemy.

conspirators People who join together to carry out an illegal act.

detonate To cause to blow up.

diplomat A person hired to negotiate, or work between, two nations.

double agent A spy pretending to serve one government while actually serving another.

embassy An office or building where diplomats conduct business.

espionage The use of spies to obtain information.

forge To make or imitate falsely.

guillotine A machine with a sharp, heavy blade used to behead people.

informants People who provide information, usually of a secret nature.

intrigue A secret scheme or plan.

malaria A disease caused by parasites, often transmitted by mosquitoes.

Morse code A code using dots or dashes to transfer information.

neutral Taking no sides in a dispute or war.

occupy To take over or control another country during a war.

optimistic Looking for the best possible outcome.

reparations Money or goods given to a winning nation by a defeated nation.

smuggle To secretly carry goods or information.

undergrowth Thick bushes or trees.

For More Information

Central Intelligence Agency
Office of Public Affairs
Washington, DC 20505
(703) 482-0623
Web site: http://www.cia.gov

Imperial War Museum
Lambeth Road
London SE1 6HZ
England
e-mail: mail@iwm.org.uk
Web site: http://www.iwm.org/uk

International Spy Museum
800 F Street NW
Washington, DC 20004
(202) 393-7798
Web site: http://www.spymuseum.org/index.asp

Museum of World War II
46 Eliot Street
Natick, MA 01760
(508) 651-7695
Web site: http://www.museumofworldwarii.com

National Women's History Museum
P.O. Box 1296
Annandale, VA 22003
(703) 813-6209
e-mail: info@nwhm.org
Web site: http://www.nmwh.org

WEB SITES
Due to the changing nature of Internet links, the
Rosen Publishing Group, Inc., has developed an
online list of Web sites related to the subject of
this book. This site is updated regularly. Please use
this link to access the list:

http://www.rosenlinks.com/aww/wwot

For Further Reading

Aline, Countess of Romanones. *The Spy Wore Red: My Adventures as an Undercover Agent in World War II.* New York: Random House, 1987.

Baker, Josephine, and Jo Bouillon. *Josephine.* Translated by Mariana Fitzpatrick. New York: Marlowe & Company, 1977.

Bancroft, Mary. *Autobiography of a Spy.* New York: William Morrow and Company, Inc., 1983.

Fitch, Noel Riley. *Appetite for Life: The Biography of Julia Child.* New York: Doubleday, 1997.

Hyde, H. Montgomery. *Cynthia.* New York: Farrar, Straus and Giroux, 1965.

Kaminski, Theresa. *Prisoners in Paradise: American Women in the Wartime South Pacific.* Lawrence, KS: University Press of Kansas, 2000.

Lovell, Mary S. *Cast No Shadow: The Life of the American Spy Who Changed the Course of World War II.* New York: Pantheon Books, 1992.

Mahoney, M. H. *Women in Espionage: A Biographical Dictionary.* Santa Barbara, CA: ABC-CLIO, Inc., 1993.

McCarthy, Linda. *Spies, Pop Flies, and French Fries: Stories I Told My Favorite Visitors to the CIA Exhibit Center.* Markham, VA: History Is a Hoot, Inc., 1999.

McIntosh, Elizabeth P. *Sisterhood of Spies: The Women of the OSS.* Annapolis, MD: Naval Institute Press, 1998.

Melton, H. Keith. *The Ultimate Spy Book.* New York: DK Publishing, Inc., 1996.

Mulrine, Anna. "The Power of Secrets." *U.S. News and World Report,* January 27–February 3, 2003, pp. 48–49.

Platt, Richard. *Spy.* New York: Alfred A. Knopf, 1996.

Sheehan, Sean. *WWII: Germany and Japan Attack.* Austin, TX: Raintree/Steck-Vaughn Publishers, 2001.

Vail, John J. *World War II: The War in Europe.* San Diego: Lucent Books, 1991.

Volkman, Ernest. *Spies: The Secret Agents Who Changed the Course of History.* New York: John Wiley & Sons, Inc., 1994.

Bibliography

Aline, Countess of Romanones. *The Spy Wore Red: My Adventures as an Undercover Agent in World War II.* New York: Random House, 1987.

Baker, Jean-Claude, and Chris Chase. *Josephine: The Hungry Heart.* New York: Random House, 1993.

Baker, Josephine, and Jo Bouillon. *Josephine.* Translated by Mariana Fitzpatrick. New York: Marlowe & Company, 1977.

Bancroft, Mary. *Autobiography of a Spy.* New York: William Morrow and Company, Inc., 1983.

Breuer, William B. *The Great Raid on Cabanatuan: Rescuing the Doomed Ghosts of Bataan and Corregidor.* New York: John Wiley & Sons, 1994.

Casey, Dr. Dennis. "Limping Lady Begins Spy Career in Early 1940s." 2003. Retrieved February 21, 2003 (http://www.64-baker-street.org/agent_others_virginia_hall.html).

Central Intelligence Agency. "The Office of Strategic Services: America's First Intelligence Agency." 2000. Retrieved March 2, 2003 (http://www.cia.gov/cia/publications/oss/).

Fitch, Noel Riley. *Appetite for Life: The Biography of Julia Child.* New York: Doubleday, 1997.

Gruhzit-Hoyt, Olga. *They Also Served: American Women in World War II.* New York: Carol Publishing Group, 1995.

Hyde, H. Montgomery. *Cynthia.* New York: Farrar, Straus and Giroux, 1965.

Kaminski, Theresa. *Prisoners in Paradise: American Women in the Wartime South Pacific.* Lawrence, KS: University Press of Kansas, 2000.

Lovell, Mary S. *Cast No Shadow: The Life of the American Spy Who Changed the Course of World War II.* New York: Pantheon Books, 1992.

Mahoney, M. H. *Women in Espionage: A Biographical Dictionary.* Santa Barbara, CA: ABC-CLIO, Inc., 1993.

Marrin, Albert. *The Secret Armies: Spies, Counterspies, and Saboteurs in World War II.* New York: Atheneum, 1985.

McCarthy, Linda. *Spies, Pop Flies, and French Fries: Stories I Told My Favorite Visitors to the CIA Exhibit Center.* Markham, VA: History Is a Hoot, Inc., 1999.

McIntosh, Elizabeth P. *Sisterhood of Spies: The Women of the OSS.* Annapolis, MD: Naval Institute Press, 1998.

Melton, H. Keith. *The Ultimate Spy Book.* New York: DK Publishing, Inc., 1996.

Mulrine, Anna. "The Power of Secrets." *U.S. News and World Report,* January 27–February 3, 2003, pp. 48–49.

O'Toole, G. J. A. *Honorable Treachery: A History of U.S. Intelligence, Espionage, and Covert Action from the American Revolution to the CIA.* New York: The Atlantic Monthly Press, 1991.

Phillips, Claire, and Myron B. Goldsmith. *Manila Espionage.* Portland, OR: Binfords & Mort, 1947.

Phillips, Claire, as told to Frederick C. Painton. "I Was an American Spy." *American Mercury* 60, May 1945, pp. 592–598.

Rose, Phyllis. *Jazz Cleopatra: Josephine Baker in Her Time.* New York: Doubleday, 1989.

Rossiter, Margaret L. *Women in the Resistance.* New York: Praeger, 1986.

Rowan, Richard Wilmer, with Robert G. Deindorfer. *Secret Service: Thirty-Three Centuries of Espionage.* New York: Hawthorn Books, Inc., 1967.

Sheehan, Sean. *WWII: Germany and Japan Attack.* Austin, TX: Raintree/Steck-Vaughn Publishers, 2001.

Sides, Hampton. *Ghost Soldiers: The Forgotten Epic Story of World War II's Most Dramatic Mission.* New York: Doubleday, 2001.

Singer, Kurt. *Spy Stories from Asia.* New York: Wilfred Funk, Inc., 1955.

Smith, R. Harris. *OSS: The Secret History of America's First Central Intelligence Agency.* Berkeley, CA: The University of California Press, 1972.

Sullivan, George. *In the Line of Fire: Eight Women War Spies.* New York: Scholastic, Inc., 1996.

Vail, John J. *World War II: The War in Europe*. San Diego: Lucent Books, 1991.

Volkman, Ernest. *Spies: The Secret Agents Who Changed the Course of History*. New York: John Wiley & Sons, Inc., 1994.

Source Notes

Introduction
1. Albert Marrin, *The Secret Armies: Spies, Counterspies, and Saboteurs in World War II* (New York: Atheneum, 1985), p. 106.
2. Ibid., p. 98.

Chapter 1
1. Linda McCarthy, *Spies, Pop Flies, and French Fries: Stories I Told My Favorite Visitors to the CIA Exhibit Center* (Markham, VA: History Is a Hoot, Inc., 1999), p. 45.
2. Margaret L. Rossiter, *Women in the Resistance* (New York: Praeger, 1986), p. 190.
3. Ibid., p. 191.
4. Elizabeth P. McIntosh, *Sisterhood of Spies: The Women of the OSS* (Annapolis, MD: Naval Institute Press, 1998), p. 114.
5. Rossiter, p. 197.
6. Ibid., pp. 197–198.
7. McIntosh, p. 122.
8. McCarthy, p. 48.

Chapter 2
1. Claire Phillips, as told to Frederick C. Painton, "I Was an American Spy" (*American Mercury*, May 1945), p. 592.
2. Claire Phillips and Myron B. Goldsmith, *Manila Espionage* (Portland, OR: Binfords & Mort, 1947), p. 82.

3. Ibid., p. 105.
4. Phillips and Painton, p. 594.
5. Phillips and Goldsmith, p. 121.
6. Ibid., p. 113.
7. Ibid., p. 128.
8. William B. Breuer, *The Great Raid on Cabanatuan: Rescuing the Doomed Ghosts of Bataan and Corregidor* (New York: John Wiley & Sons, 1994), p. 107.
9. Phillips and Goldsmith, p. 171.
10. Ibid., p. 198.
11. Ibid., p. 201.

Chapter 3

1. Aline, Countess of Romanones, *The Spy Wore Red: My Adventures as an Undercover Agent in World War II* (New York: Random House, 1987), p. 84.
2. Ibid., p. 203.
3. Ibid., p. 246.

Chapter 4

1. H. Montgomery Hyde, *Cynthia* (New York: Farrar, Straus and Giroux, 1965), p. 16.
2. Ernest Volkman, *Spies: The Secret Agents Who Changed the Course of History* (New York: John Wiley & Sons, Inc., 1994), p. 108.
3. Mary S. Lovell, *Cast No Shadow: The Life of the American Spy Who Changed the Course of World War II* (New York: Pantheon Books, 1992), p. 135.
4. Donald Downes, *The Scarlet Thread* (London: Verschoyle, 1953), pp. 59–60.
5. Ibid.
6. Elizabeth P. McIntosh, *Sisterhood of Spies: The Women of the OSS* (Annapolis, MD: Naval Institute Press, 1998), p. 24.
7. Lovell, p. 225.

8. Ibid., p. 229.
9. Hyde, p. 204.
10. Lovell, p. 240.

Chapter 5

1. Jean-Claude Baker and Chris Chase, *Josephine: The Hungry Heart* (New York: Random House, 1993), p. 227.
2. Josephine Baker and Jo Bouillon, *Josephine* (New York: Marlowe & Company, 1977), p. 124.
3. Ibid., p. 125.
4. Ibid.

Chapter 6

1. Mary Bancroft, *Autobiography of a Spy* (New York: William Morrow and Company, Inc., 1983), p. 8.
2. Ibid., p. 7.
3. Ibid., p. 7.
4. Ibid., p. 150.
5. Ibid., p. 162.
6. Ibid., p. 207.
7. Ibid., pp. 291–292.
8. Elizabeth P. McIntosh, *Sisterhood of Spies: The Women of the OSS* (Annapolis, MD: Naval Institute Press, 1998), p. 182.

Conclusion

1. Linda McCarthy, *Spies, Pop Flies, and French Fries: Stories I Told My Favorite Visitors to the CIA Exhibit Center* (Markham, VA: History Is a Hoot, Inc., 1999), p. 45.

Index

Acknowledgments

The author would like to thank Howard Cooper, Lori Cooper, and Marina Lang for their valuable insights, suggestions, and continued support. She would also like to thank the reference librarians of the Boston Public Library and the Wakefield (Massachusetts) Public Library for their assistance.

About the Author

Simone Payment has a degree in psychology from Cornell University and a master's degree in elementary education from Wheelock College. She is the author of six books for young adults.

Photo Credits

Front cover, pp. 20, 56 © AP/Wide World Photos; back cover courtesy of Record Group 226 (OSS), National Archives and Records Administration, College Park, MD; p. 5 © Popperfoto/Retrofile.com; pp. 7, 16, 43, 47, 54, 64, 65, 68, 72, 87, 89 © Hulton Archive/Getty Images; pp. 10, 28–29 Still Picture Branch, National Archives and Records Administration; pp. 22, 23, 24 (right and left), 32, 60 © Bettmann/Corbis; pp. 27, 36, 80 © Corbis; p. 40 © Culver Pictures; p. 49 © AFP/Corbis; pp. 70, 76 © Hulton-Deutsch Collection/Corbis; p. 82 Princeton University Library; p. 85 © Ullstein Bild, Berlin; pp. 92–93 © Roger Ressmeyer/Corbis.

Designer: Evelyn Horovicz, **Editor:** Charles Hofer; **Photo Researcher:** Peter Tomlinson